W9-AWC-756

East Jackson Elementary
Media Center
1531 Hoods Mill Rd
Commerce, GA 30529

20TH CENTURY USA

History
of the
1990s

Rennay Craats

WEIGL PUBLISHERS INC.

Published by Weigl Publishers Inc.
123 South Broad Street, Box 227
Mankato, MN, USA
Web site: http://www.weigl.com

Copyright © 2002 WEIGL PUBLISHERS INC.
All rights reserved. No part of this publication may be reproduced, stored in
a retrieval system, or transmitted in any form or by any means, electronic,
mechanical, photocopying, recording, or otherwise, without the prior written
permission of Weigl Publishers Inc.

Library of Congress Cataloging-in-Publication Data available upon request
from the publisher. Fax (507) 388-2746 for the attention of the Publishing
Records Department.

ISBN 1-930954-44-1

Printed and bound in the United States of America
1 2 3 4 5 6 7 8 9 0   05 04 03 02 01

Senior Editor
Jared Keen

Series Editor
Carlotta Lemieux

Layout and Design
Warren Clark
Carla Pelky

Copy Editor
Jay Winans

Photo Research
Angela Lowen
Joe Nelson

Photograph Credits

AFP/CORBIS: Page 9; Archive Photos: Page 24; SAGA/Frank Capri/Archive Photos: Pages 3BL,
25; Reuters/Lee Celano/Archive Photos: Pages 31, 33; Jacques M. Chenet/CORBIS: Page 32;
CNP/Archive Photos: Pages 6BL, 16, 20; Digital Vision: Page 15; Bill Gentile/CORBIS: Page
38; Scott Harrison/Archive Photos: Pages 3MR, 41; International/Archive Photos: Pages 7BR,
40; Earl & Nazima Kowall/CORBIS: Page 19; Reuters/John Kuntz/Archive Photos: Page 8;
John K. Marshall: Page 37; Wally McNamee/CORBIS: Page 34; Reuters/Win McNamee/Archive
Photos: Page 22; MPI: Pages 6BR, 18; NASA: Pages 26, 27; Photofest: pages 3TL, 10, 11,
12, 13, 14, 28, 36; Reuters/Vincenzo Pinto/Archive Photos: Page 30; Ron Sachs/CNP/Archive
Photos: Page 21; Reuters/Blake Sell/Archive Photos: Pages 7BL, 39; ChromoSohm Inc./
CORBIS: Page 35; Reuters/Stringer/Archive Photos: Page 23; Reuters/Ray Stubblebine/Archive
Photos: Page 29; David & Peter Turnley/CORBIS: Pages 17, 42, 43.

Every reasonable effort has been made to trace ownership and to obtain permission to reprint
copyright material. The publishers would be pleased to have any errors or omissions brought
to their attention so that they may be corrected in subsequent printings.

USA 1990s Contents

Entertainment 10

Literature 24

Music 40

Million Man March

Desert Storm

Waco Standoff

TITANIC

Hubble Telescope

Wrestlemania

The Bush Years

Free Trade

Rodney King

Oklahoma City Bombing

The last decade of the century was one of changes, events, and advances. Americans celebrated the accomplishments of sports heroes, award-winning authors, and political leaders.

Michael Jordan captivated audiences on the basketball court, Venus Williams took the tennis world by storm, and Tiger Woods raised golf to a new level. Americans spent their leisure time reading John Grisham's exciting courtroom dramas or escaped into Danielle Steel's romantic tales. Citizens watched as President Clinton helped maintain democracy and peace around the world. Science carried people to where they had never before been. Transplants and new medical methods saved lives and gave people hope. Computer technology took off, and Americans could communicate with people across the globe with the click of a mouse.

The nineties was also a tough decade for many Americans. The technology people embraced, along with a faltering economy, caused companies to cut their number of employees. Many Americans lost their jobs because of this **downsizing**. The country also

Body Piercing

Inline Skating

Harry Potter

Backstreet Boys

Swissair Tragedy

Coastal Quake

SCHOOL SHOOTING

Seinfeld a Smash

Tiger Woods

experienced episodes of terrible violence. The Oklahoma City bombing shocked Americans, and the Rodney King beating caused riots throughout America. The Columbine shooting made people think differently about guns and children, but people did not lose hope. They came together and rebuilt their lives and their communities. By the end of the decade, new

laws were in place to curb violence, and the economy was enjoying a period of growth and prosperity.

Not everything that happened in the decade could be covered in *20th Century USA: History of the 1990s*. It is a collection of just some of the fascinating events that shaped history. Your local library and the Internet are great places to learn about the

aftermaths of these events. You can also find out more about the history of the decade by exploring old newspapers and magazines. For now, turn the page and find out about the final, exciting decade of the twentieth century—the 1990s.

1990

Kevin Costner dances with wolves in a film like no other. The authentic tale of Native Americans captured the imaginations and attention of audiences. Find out why on page 12.

1990

Saddam Hussein moves into Kuwait. He goes too far. The invasion draws criticism and action from other countries. Find out more about the invasion and the reaction to it on page 17.

1991

The U.S. military takes action in the Middle East. It is sent in to force Iraq from Kuwait. Find out about President Bush's decision to act on page 20.

1991

Four Los Angeles police officers set off riots and racial tension after beating an African-American man. The video tape of the beating adds fuel to the fire. Page 33 has the details about Rodney King's ordeal.

1991

Anthony Hopkins terrifies big-screen audiences. His performance as Hannibal Lechter helps *The Silence of the Lambs* earn an Academy Award. Page 10 has the scoop.

1992

A billionaire from Texas enters the race for the presidency. He receives more votes than any independent candidate had in the past eighty years. Page 22 has the story of Ross Perot.

1992

Bosnia declares its independence. This only leads to more violence in the former Yugoslavia. Find out about the horrible conflict on page 17.

1993

After forty-nine straight days of rain, the Midwest is ravaged by floods. Fifty people die, and thousands are left homeless. Page 9 has the details.

1993

Israel and Palestine take a step toward peace. The two rivals shake hands and sign an agreement. Find out what they agreed to and how it turned out on page 18.

1994

Who would have imagined that figure skating could be so competitive and so violent? Tonya Harding will not let anything or anyone stand in the way of her quest for Olympic gold. Find out what she did to increase her chances of success on page 29.

1994

All eyes are on the First Family. A scandal surrounding a real estate company and a savings and loan association threatens President Clinton's administration. Read more about Whitewater on page 23.

Desert Storm

Rodney King protest

1994

Television audiences go crazy for the antics of six New Yorkers. *Friends* hits the top of the ratings. To find out more about the characters and the success of the sitcom, turn to page 13.

1995

A rented truck and fertilizer change life in Oklahoma City, and the U.S., forever. A bomb blast kills innocent people and shocks the world. Find out more about the explosion that was felt around the country on page 8.

1995

The *Galileo* **probe** descends into Jupiter's atmosphere. Find out more about its journey on page 26.

1995

The country is split over the guilt or innocence of O. J. Simpson. The trial of the century raises issues of domestic violence and racism. Find out how the trial ended on page 32.

1996

Thousands of people are becoming U.S. citizens. Texas and California host enormous **naturalization** ceremonies. Find out about the increase in citizenship on page 39.

1996

All hail the kings of the diamond. The New York Yankees reclaim their place in the sun with a World Series victory. Read more about the team on page 29.

1997

Diana, Princess of Wales, is dead. The world mourns the loss of the people's princess and points a finger at photographers. Find out why on page 19.

Galileo probe

1998

Swissair flight 111 comes crashing into the ocean. No one survives the crash. Read about the last moments aboard the ill-fated airplane on page 19.

1998

A wrestler and movie actor settles into the top political position in the state. Find out how "The Body" became Minnesota's governor on page 22.

1998

The ship sank, but the movie stayed afloat. *Titanic* causes a sensation around the world. Turn to page 11 to read about the stupendous film based on a real-life tragedy.

1999

Two teenagers walk into their school with weapons and start firing. The tragedy devastates the country. Read more about the terrible shooting at Columbine High School on page 8.

1999

A U.S. man is given a hand, literally. Doctors perform the first hand transplant in America. Find out more on page 27.

1999

Lauryn Hill's unbeatable voice launches her to the top of the charts. She takes home armfuls of awards in recognition of her success. Find out more on page 40.

1999

The Kennedy curse claims another member of Camelot. John F. Kennedy, Jr., is killed in a plane crash. Find out about him and other victims of the so-called curse on page 33.

1999

An exhausted Lance Armstrong claims one of the toughest cycling victories ever—the Tour de France. Find out what made his victory even more amazing on page 30.

Lauryn Hill

Bombing Rocks the Country

On the morning of April 19, 1995, a car bomb changed the lives of Oklahomans. People were dropping off their children at daycare or arriving at work at the Alfred P. Murrah Federal Building in Oklahoma City. A rental truck parked out front exploded at 9:03 AM, causing the front half of the nine-story building to collapse. The bomb was an estimated 1,000 to 1,200 pounds, and the blast was heard 30 miles away. For two weeks, rescue crews searched for survivors. People were buried under piles of steel and concrete. The rest of the country was glued to television broadcasts that gave details and tallied the death toll. After the dust had settled, 168 men, women, and children were dead. Hundreds more were injured. It was the worst act of **terrorism** in the U.S. Investigations revealed that the bomb was unsophisticated, made

"It was just like an atomic bomb went off. The ceiling went in, and all the windows came in, and there was a deafening roar."

An Oklahoma City bombing survivor

■ There was a great outpouring of support for the victims of the Oklahoma City bombing.

from a mixture of fertilizer and fuel oil.

An hour after the bomb exploded, a 27-year-old man named Timothy McVeigh was pulled over for driving without a license plate. He was supposed to be released on April 21, but he became the bombing suspect. He

was charged, along with his friend, Terry Nichols. Another man, Michael Fortier, pleaded guilty to lesser charges and testified against the others. Nichols was sentenced to life in prison, and McVeigh received a death sentence. McVeigh was executed on June 11, 2001.

Terror at Columbine

A shooting rampage in Columbine, Colorado, on April 20, 1999, left fifteen people dead. What made this event more horrifying was that it occurred at a high school, and the gunmen were students. Eric Harris and Dylan Klebold came to school heavily armed. They approached the school with rifles, pistols, shotguns, and bombs, and began

shooting as they walked inside. About 1,500 students escaped from the school when the firing started. Other students and teachers hid inside, afraid to move. The gunmen continued to fire at anyone they encountered as they walked down the hall, through the cafeteria, and upstairs to the library. Harris and Klebold also fired at rescue workers and police outside. Some accounts estimate that about 900 rounds of ammunition

were emptied at Columbine High School. At the end of the massacre, the two boys turned their weapons on themselves. Twelve students and one teacher were shot to death by these two troubled students. Another twenty-three students and faculty members were seriously injured. The country was shocked that this could happen, and people from coast to coast mourned the deaths.

Coastal Quake

Early on January 17, 1994, the event that California had dreaded occurred—the ground began to shake. It began in the Los Angeles neighborhood of Northridge, where an apartment complex toppled under the earthquake's power. Sixteen people in the building were killed. Across the city, homes, schools, businesses, and churches were destroyed. Freeways and roadways collapsed, trapping and even killing motorists in their vehicles. Eleven of the roadways, which residents and emergency crews usually relied on, were too heavily damaged to be used.

While this quake was likely not the "Big One" that geologists had warned of, it was still very destructive. It caused $15 billion in damage and killed fifty-seven people. It also took a toll on the residents of Los Angeles—some decided to move to safer areas of the country.

Compound Standoff

A religious group called the Branch Davidians set up its headquarters in Waco, Texas. The group's leader, Vernon Howell, took the name David Koresh— "David" for the kingdom of David and "Koresh" from the Hebrew name of a Persian king who freed the Jews from Babylon. Koresh preached about the end of the world, and he warned of evil that would descend on their compound. To prepare for this, he and his followers collected food, weapons, and fuel. In 1993, the Federal Bureau of Alcohol, Tobacco, and Firearms (ATF) raided the compound. On February 28, agents arrived

■ An investigation into the Waco siege cleared the federal agents involved of any wrongdoing.

with warrants to search for illegal weapons. They were met with gunfire. Four agents died and another sixteen were wounded in the shootout. Several Branch Davidians were also killed or wounded, although the number is unknown.

The shooting resulted in a fifty-one-day standoff between the agents and the Davidians. Then, on April 19, the agents advanced. They fired tear gas into the buildings to try to force the members out. Soon afterward, a fire broke out that quickly consumed the wooden

MIDWEST UNDER WATER

■ In the summer of 1993, rain pounded the Midwest for forty-nine straight days. The Mississippi River and its tributaries burst over the banks and the levees, rushing into farms and towns. Damage to the area was estimated at $15 billion, and about 10,000 homes were destroyed. Farmland was soaked—at least 15 million acres were flooded. It would take years before the land was usable again. The flooding had a huge human cost as well. Fifty people died in the flooding, and thousands of others had to leave their homes. It took months before some of these residents could return to their houses. The 1993 flood was one of the largest and most expensive natural disasters ever.

buildings. The agents claimed that the Davidians had started the fire themselves, but supporters of the sect insisted that the blaze had been set by the agents' assault. After the fire, eighty bodies were found. It was one of the worst acts of peacetime violence in U.S. history.

RE-RELEASE HITS TOP

■ Twenty years after it was released in theaters, *Star Wars* hit the top of the box office again. A re-release of the sci-fi classic in 1997 earned $35.9 million in the U.S. in the first weekend alone. The other movies in the series—*The Empire Strikes Back* and *The Return of the Jedi*—were also re-released to packed theaters. Director George Lucas spent $10 million improving the special effects in the movies, and he included clips that did not appear in the original releases. With the new boost in ticket sales, *Star Wars* became the biggest all-time U.S. domestic box-office hit.

Lucas had more up his sleeve than re-releases. He was getting audiences ready for a new *Star Wars* movie. *Episode One: The Phantom Menace* was a **prequel** to the 1977 *Star Wars*. This 1999 movie presented Luke Skywalker's father as a 9-year-old boy with incredible Jedi promise, and Obi-Wan Kenobi as a young Jedi warrior. Other familiar, though much younger, characters appeared in the prequel, including Yoda, R2-D2, and Jabba the Hutt. People lined up for days to watch the premiere of *Episode One: The Phantom Menace*. Audiences could not get enough of the *Star Wars* gang, and were eagerly awaiting Lucas's next installment.

Silence of the Lambs

Most often, thriller movies are absent from the Academy's Oscar nomination list. *Silence of the Lambs* became the exception in 1991. The psychological horror movie followed special agent Clarice Starling, played by Jodie Foster, as she tried to find a serial killer. She looked to the imprisoned cannibal Hannibal Lechter for insight. Hannibal, played by Anthony Hopkins, possessed charm, confidence, and calculated evil.

The performances of Foster and Hopkins were incredible, and the non-stop suspense and action kept audiences on the edge of their seats. The clever twists of plot were what earned it the Academy Award for Best Picture. A sequel to *Silence of the Lambs*, called *Hannibal*, was released in 2001.

There's Johnny

After thirty years as the king of late-night television, Johnny Carson sat behind *The Tonight Show* desk for the last time on May 22, 1992. He had hosted more than 4,500 episodes of the talk show and won numerous awards, including four Emmys, the American Comedy Lifetime Achievement Award in 1992, and the 1993 Kennedy Center Lifetime Achievement Award. Over the years, Carson had made characters such as "Aunt Blabby" and "Carnac the Magnificent" much-loved parts of late-night entertainment. *The Tonight Show* also showcased young comedians. When Carson liked the comedian, he called the performer over for a chat—the comedian had officially made it. Carson launched the careers of many well-known comedians, including Ellen Degeneres and Jeff Foxworthy.

When Carson could not host *The Tonight Show*, he called on several guest hosts to fill in. Jay Leno took over for Joan Rivers as permanent guest host in the late 1980s, and Leno was also chosen to host the show when Carson retired. Carson's last show looked back over the years and highlighted hilarious moments from his time as host. People across the country were sad that Johnny Carson would no longer be part of their bedtime ritual. At the time of his retirement, Carson was the highest paid television personality in history, earning about $2,380 per minute of airtime.

■ Johnny Carson first appeared on *The Tonight Show* on October 2, 1962.

Titanic Movie

More than eighty years after the unsinkable ship sank, director James Cameron filmed a movie about the ill-fated liner. In 1998, *Titanic* hit the big screen. The story was a true account of the disastrous first voyage of the ship, combined with the fictional love story of two young people aboard the *Titanic*. When doing research for the film, Cameron sent remote control cameras to the wreckage of the actual *Titanic* at the bottom of the ocean to record how it looked. He wanted to include authentic design details in his movie. To say the film was a sensation would be an understatement. The performances of Kate Winslet and Leonardo Di Caprio, along with the breathtaking photography, kept audiences glued to their seats and kept the film at number one at the box office for a record fifteen weeks. *Titanic* was nominated for fourteen Academy Awards and walked away with eleven Oscars, including Best Picture, Best Director, Best Costume Design, and Best Visual Effects. The film also won Golden Globe Awards for Best Film (Drama), Best Directing, Best Original Score, and Best Original Song. *Titanic* earned $1.8 billion at box offices around the world and another $250 million in movie rentals or video purchases in the first week of its release. The film renewed interest in the 1912 disaster, giving rise to *Titanic* sightseeing tours, souvenirs, and visits to the graves of the victims.

■ *Titanic* cost more than $200 million to make.

Hollywood Hero

Tom Hanks began his career as a comedian. He appeared in television sitcoms until he got his break with the 1984 hit *Splash!* In 1988, his role in *Big* earned him an Academy Award nomination for Best Actor. In 1992, Hanks played a rude, crude, washed-up baseball player hired to coach a women's team during World War II. *A League of their Own* was a huge success, and it led to another role in a hit romantic comedy, *Sleepless in Seattle*. Many fans thought Hanks was a great comedian, but they doubted that he could succeed in dramatic roles. He proved them wrong in 1993 with his portrayal of a lawyer with AIDS in *Philadelphia*. The performance earned Hanks an Academy Award for Best Actor. His trip to the Oscars became a habit when he again won the award for Best Actor for his role in *Forrest Gump* the following year.

Hanks could not avoid success. The story of *Apollo 13* hit the big screen in 1995 to rave reviews. Then the Hollywood legend took up directing, winning Emmys for his television miniseries *From Earth to the Moon*. In 1998, he was back in front of the camera in *Saving Private Ryan*, which was nominated for eleven Academy Awards, including one for Hanks. He returned to his comedy roots with the smash hit *You've Got Mail*.

His vast success in movies has made Hanks one of the top movie celebrities of all time.

CRIME DRAMA A HIT

■ The crime drama *Law & Order* debuted on October 30, 1990. Through its complex stories, *Law & Order* showed the ins and outs of the legal system. Many of the plots were drawn from the unbelievable real-life events highlighted in newspaper headlines. Each week, more than 16 million people tuned in to watch Lennie Briscoe, played by Jerry Orbach, and Edward Green, played by Jesse L. Martin, investigate crimes. Abbie Carmichael, played by Angie Harmon, and Jack McCoy, played by Sam Waterston, prosecuted the suspects. *Law & Order* received a record nine Emmy nominations for Outstanding Drama Series, and it won the honor in 1997. With its renewal until at least 2005, the program became the longest-running police series on television and the second-longest running drama series.

■ Julia Roberts had been twice nominated for an Academy Award before her triumph as Erin Brokovich.

America's Sweetheart

Julia Roberts used her southern charm and wholesomeness to break into Hollywood. Her talent kept her there. She got her break in the 1988 film *Satisfaction*. From there she moved from movie to movie, appearing in *Mystic Pizza* (1989), *Steel Magnolias* (1989)—for which she won a Golden Globe for Best Supporting Actress—and *Flatliners* (1990). *Flatliners* was a star-studded film, boosting Roberts into the ranks of Kiefer Sutherland and Kevin Bacon. It was the 1990 blockbuster, *Pretty Woman*, with Richard Gere, that put Roberts on the map. It also earned her a Best Actress Oscar nomination and a Golden Globe award for Best Actress in a Musical or Comedy. Despite her instant fame, her next films did not draw audiences, and she stepped back from acting. In 1993, Roberts's career took off again with the release of *The Pelican Brief*. Playing a sassy law student, she stole the show. After a few more box-office flops, Roberts got back on top with her roles in *Michael Collins* and *Conspiracy Theory* in 1996. There was no stopping her from there. Her performances in *My Best Friend's Wedding*, *Runaway Bride*, and *Notting Hill* made her a favorite of U.S. audiences and producers everywhere. In 2000, Roberts received the highest salary ever paid to a screen actress for the lead role in *Erin Brokovich* (2000). Roberts was paid $20 million and earned an Academy Award for Best Actress.

Dances with Oscars

Kevin Costner revived the western movie in 1990 and, at the same time, reversed the role of "good guys" from cowboys to Native Americans. Costner directed, co-produced, and starred in the three-hour film *Dances with Wolves*. The film was about a Civil War-era soldier and his experiences living alone in Native land. The scenery and filming were awe-inspiring. Also, rather than having Native Americans speaking English, Costner had them speaking in the Lakota language. Costner's character, soldier John Dunbar, explored nature and was seen dancing in the middle of the open prairies with a wolf he named Two Socks. When Dunbar was befriended by a Sioux tribe, he was given the name Dances with Wolves for this action. Dunbar left his old world behind and joined the Sioux people. *Dances with Wolves* was a huge success with the public and was a hit with the Academy as well. It won seven Academy Awards, including one for Best Picture, Best Editing, and Best Director.

The Show about Nothing

*S*einfeld had critics and viewers doubled over with laughter every week. In 1998, after nine seasons on the air, "the show about nothing" aired its final episode. Fans were upset that no new shows of the everyday adventures of George, Jerry, Elaine, and Kramer would be created. Such episodes as those featuring "The Soup Nazi" and "Bubble Boy" became part of nineties culture. The show was the most successful and most watched program of the 1990s, earning many Emmy Awards and $200 million in profits. Products,

"This show has been the greatest love affair of my life. But we were all together on it. We all felt we wanted to leave in love."

Jerry Seinfeld

including clothing, posters, and cards, exploded into stores, and viewers scooped them up. In the end, the show's namesake, Jerry Seinfeld, wanted to end the series on a high note. Not even a reported $5 million per episode from NBC would change his mind. After all, in 1996, he earned $94 million and was paid $1 million per episode in 1997. The rest of the cast agreed, and they took their final bows in May 1998.

■ About 76 million people tuned in to watch the final episode of *Seinfeld.*

Thursday Night Friends

O n September 22, 1994, television audiences were invited into the lives of six hilarious people. *Friends* was an instant success. The half-hour sitcom featured the antics of New Yorkers Phoebe (Lisa Kudrow), Monica (Courtney Cox Arquette), Rachel (Jennifer Aniston), Chandler (Matthew Perry), Ross (David Schwimmer), and Joey (Matt LeBlanc). The characters had quirks that entertained and endeared them to audiences.

Monica was a chef with a need for neatness; Chandler's dry sense of humor and fear of commitment made him a favorite of fans; Joey was a struggling actor who made up for his dim wits with a handsome face; Rachel worked in fashion and was searching for Mr. Right; Ross was a paleontologist turned professor who had been unlucky in marriage three times; and Phoebe brought her offbeat ideas and otherworldly experiences to the circle of friends.

Since the first season, the show earned twenty-seven Emmy Award nominations, including four for Outstanding Comedy

Series. The actors won a Screen Guild Award for Outstanding Ensemble Performance in a Comedy Series in 1996, and they were nominated three times for the Golden Globe's Best Television Series. The people showed their approval by awarding *Friends* the Favorite New Comedy Series at the People's Choice Awards and by voting for two more awards for Favorite Comedy Series. At the end of the decade, the show was going strong, despite contract and salary disputes. *Friends* was the number one comedy and top-rated 8 PM series on television.

Cartoons Get Respect

In the 1990s, cartoons were no longer reserved for children on Saturday mornings. Cartoon feature films were reaching a new level of respect in Hollywood. In 1991, *Beauty and the Beast* astonished audiences with its incredible music and the realistic animation. The film was nominated for an Academy Award for Best Picture. It was the first time that a cartoon had reached that level of success. Other Disney films, including *The Little Mermaid, Aladdin*, and *The Lion King*, became hits with both children and parents.

Television also picked up on the animation trend, but its cartoons were made for adults. *The Simpsons* was an adult cartoon about a family of misfits. Bart, the young boy, was always in trouble and was quick with insults. Lisa was a scholar who did not fit in with her family. Homer, their father, was dim-witted and loved donuts. Marg, the mother, tried to keep her family in line, and Maggie, the baby, never said a word. *The Simpsons* was a huge hit, and its success brought more adult-focused cartoons, including *King of the Hill* and the controversial *South Park*. The language and content of many *South Park* episodes provided proof that cartoons were not just for kids.

■ *The Simpsons'* first season was in 1990.

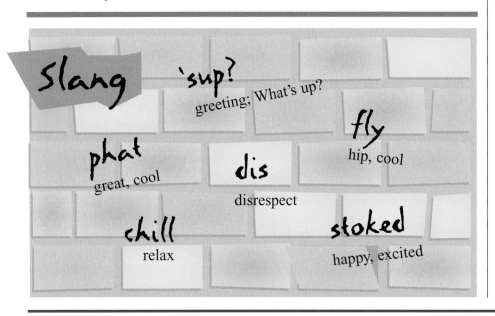

Slang

'sup? greeting; What's up?

phat great, cool

dis disrespect

fly hip, cool

chill relax

stoked happy, excited

KEEP ROLLING

■ In the 1990s, inline skating became more and more popular. People were no longer just rolling on paths and sidewalks. They used inline skates to play roller hockey. Roller hockey leagues quickly spread across the country. Inline skate parks were also introduced. This gave people a chance to try skateboarding tricks on inline skates, and skaters used rails, boxes, stairs, and park benches as launching pads. Some inline skaters entered races that took place over many miles. There seemed no end to what Americans could do on inline skates. One thing they could do, unfortunately, was fall. Hospitals were filled with broken wrists, muscle pulls, and cuts and bruises from spills taken while inline skating. This led to a push for safe skating. Safety organizations encouraged skaters to wear helmets and wrist, knee, and elbow guards to prevent serious injuries. The message was generally well received, and Americans continued to enjoy inline skating into the twenty-first century.

Coffee Houses

In the 1990s, Americans' heads were spinning with choices: mochaccino, cappuccino, decaf low-fat latté, and iced coffee. People were crazy for coffee. The beverage became more than just something to drink—it was a way of life. People gathered in coffee shops for business meetings or spent lazy Saturday afternoons with friends sipping fancy, and often expensive, drinks. Even those who did not have time to relax at coffee shops needed a shot of java to keep them going. Go-mugs and travel cups kept Americans in caffeine at all times. No matter where a person was, there was sure to be a coffee shop on the nearest corner. The coffee phenomenon spread to homes as well. Many Americans bought the coffee beans and special equipment that coffee shops used to make these drinks. A cappuccino machine was a must-have for many people in the 1990s. Americans spent many hours and dollars trying to brew the perfect cup of java.

Piercing What?

Traditionally, body piercing was a cultural practice. In the 1980s, it was mostly women who pierced their ears, sometimes having many piercings in one ear. By the 1990s, both males and females took part in the piercing craze. Piercings strayed from the traditional area, earlobes. They began showing up all over the body. The trend was to have metal in new areas such as eyebrows, noses, belly-buttons, tongues, and lips. Studs or rings adorned the faces of the nineties generation. Many parents thought their children's goal was to shock them, just as they had shocked their parents by wearing their hair long or their skirts short in the 1960s or 1970s. Many of the young people insisted that they were merely making fashion statements and showing their individuality with their pierced body parts. Their explanation was often not enough for parents, teachers, and employers. Many parents tried to prevent their children from getting pierced, while teachers and employers banned the rings. This did not stop the youth of the nineties. They took the rings out for their shift or during the school day and put them back in at the end of it. Body piercings were here to stay.

■ Tongue piercings were very popular in the 1990s.

TUNED IN

■ In the nineties, audiences had more television programs to choose from than ever before. By 1991, three-quarters of U.S. families had video cassette recorders (VCRs). The VCR was the fastest-selling piece of home-entertainment equipment in history. It offered a relatively inexpensive source of entertainment. More and more Americans were choosing to spend their Friday nights in front of their televisions. There were more than 4 billion movie rentals in the U.S. in 1991 alone. In some areas, movie watchers could order films from their homes.

By 1992, cable television was exploding. Revenues for this service reached $22 billion. Viewers had countless channels with hundreds of comedies, dramas, and cultural programs running twenty-four hours a day.

■ Shortly after he was elected president, Nelson Mandela developed a trade relationship with the U.S.

A New South Africa

Even from a jail cell, Nelson Mandela led the fight for equality in South Africa. The country had experienced **apartheid** since the 1940s. This meant that different races had separate schools, jobs, neighborhoods, and rights. Apartheid broke South Africa into four major categories— white, black, colored, and Asian.

Colored people were those of mixed heritage. As the decades passed, black Africans continued to rally against apartheid, but the white population had control of nearly all of the land and held powerful positions. In 1964, Mandela was sentenced to life in prison for trying to free black Africans. In the face of international criticism, the apartheid government began to change its policies in the mid-

eighties. Black labor unions were allowed to organize, and opposition to the government grew. Change was slow, but in 1990, the new president, F. W. de Klerk, announced an official end to apartheid. The African National Congress (ANC) was no longer banned, and its political leader, Mandela, was released from prison. This marked the beginning of black African politics and leadership. Mandela and de Klerk shared the Nobel Peace Prize in 1993 for their reforms. The next year, Mandela won the first multiracial election in the country. As the nation's president, he worked for equality and a stronger South Africa until he stepped down in 1997. Thabo Mbeki picked up the charge and carried on with Mandela's work.

AGREEING ON PEACE

■ After twelve years of war, there was finally peace in El Salvador. The civil war came to an end in February 1992 with an agreement between President Alfredo Cristiani's National Republic Alliance (ARENA) government and Farabundo Martí's rebels of the National Liberation Front (FMLN). The peace agreement called for an immediate cease-fire. It was

agreed that the rebels would gradually lay down their arms. The president agreed to get rid of corrupt officers in the military. The military had committed 85 percent of the war crimes—they had tortured and killed people, including priests and nuns. The president also agreed to reduce the size of the army by nearly half. He opened up the political system so that those opposed to

the government could take part. These changes took two years to complete, and the United Nations (UN) was on hand to ensure that the peace remained. Elections in 1994 lifted ARENA candidate Armando Calderón Sol to the presidency, and the FMLN guerrillas won a block of seats in the National Assembly.

EXIT THE IRON LADY

Margaret Thatcher had served her country well. When she retired as prime minister in 1990, she had been Great Britain's leader for eleven years. That was the longest term of any British prime minister. By privatizing industries, reforming the welfare system, and defending Britain's claims in the Falkland Islands, Thatcher had re-established Britain as a world power. However, her rule was marred by high unemployment, homelessness, and crime rates.

Her tax system was also criticized. She replaced property taxes with a "community charge" on services. This stiff charge applied to every adult—Thatcher opponents nicknamed it "the tax for being alive." Thatcher's popularity fell, and her opponents called for her resignation. The Conservatives chose John Major as the party leader, and he became prime minister. Despite Thatcher's flaws, she proved that a woman could run a country.

Yugoslavia in Tatters

In 1991, Slovenia and Croatia declared their independence from the Yugoslavian federation of republics. In July, Serbian armies began forcing millions of non-Serbs out of their territory in an attempt, they claimed, to protect their land. Many others were beaten, tortured, and killed. Croatians and Muslims in the area fought back with terrible violence. Within three months, this ethnic hatred erupted into civil war.

In 1992, Bosnia declared its independence. For about 500 years, its Muslim, Serbian, and Croatian population had lived relatively peacefully together. When Bosnia became an independent republic, the Serb-dominated Yugoslavian army objected and took over much of the country. The beautiful capital city, Sarajevo, was reduced to rubble. Snipers fired from rooftops, and residents hid in their basements. The UN sent

Citizens of Sarajevo survey the damage caused by civil war.

in troops to help calm the civil war. It placed **sanctions** on Serbia and launched relief campaigns for suffering victims. This was not enough. Serbian leader Slobodan Milosevic ordered the armies to clear out villages in the name of "ethnic cleansing." Soldiers killed and tortured Bosnians or imprisoned them in concentration camps. By the end of 1992, the violence on both sides had escalated. More than 1 million people had been forced from their homes, and tens of thousands were dead.

Iraq Takes Kuwait

In August 1990, Iraqi forces invaded the small but wealthy neighboring country of Kuwait. The invasion pleased the Iraqis because they had long claimed that Kuwait was part of Iraq. Saddam Hussein justified the invasion by saying that Kuwait was "stealing" billions of dollars worth of oil by taking it from land that belonged to Iraq.

Iraqi forces quickly took Kuwait. This alarmed Saudi Arabia and other countries of the Arab League. Hussein made enemies of other countries, too. He spread anti-American **propaganda.** He executed an Iranian-born British journalist, and he threatened to attack Israel with chemical weapons. The Arab League told Hussein to take his troops out of Kuwait, but he refused to do so. The U.S., Britain, and other countries agreed that he had to be stopped. President Bush pushed for military action to end Hussein's bullying. To protect Kuwait, Bush launched Operation Desert Shield. About 500,000 U.S. troops descended on the Saudi Desert and Persian Gulf. Within a few months, Desert Shield led to the offensive military action, Desert Storm.

Communism Gives Way to Democracy

Communism was chased out of the Soviet Union in August 1991 after a group of **hard-line** communists tried to oust the Soviet president, Mikhail Gorbachev. They made him a prisoner in his summer home. These hardliners were angry with Gorbachev for letting the Soviet republics become more democratic. They wanted to return to old-style communism. They failed. The president of the Russian republic, Boris Yeltsin, and tens of thousands of supporters rallied to defend democracy. They blocked the rebels from entering the parliament. The rebels realized that they had lost, and they released Gorbachev. The attempted **coup** was over and so was the communist Soviet Union. While Gorbachev was still the Soviet leader, the people looked to Yeltsin as their hero. At Yeltsin's urging, Gorbachev dissolved the Communist Party and returned the republics to their own rule. In December 1991, Gorbachev resigned as president of a country that essentially no longer existed. Meanwhile, Yeltsin was re-elected as president of the independent Russian Republic.

Israel and Palestine Shake Hands

No one thought it could ever happen. The forty-five-year-old feud between Israelis and Palestinians had run too deep. Then, in 1993, the leaders of these two sides shook hands and signed a peace agreement. Palestinian leader Yasir Arafat and Israeli Prime Minister Yitzhak Rabin met in Washington, DC, to work out a peace accord with the help of President Clinton. The September 13 meeting ended with a preliminary treaty, but that was a step in the right direction. The meeting was the most promising event in Middle East peace efforts since the 1970s.

The peace agreement allowed for five years of self-rule by Palestinians in the Gaza Strip

■ Despite the 1993 agreement, war still rages in the Middle East.

and Jericho. Israeli troops would reduce their presence on the West Bank, and elections for a Palestinian government could be held there. Israel, however, would continue to provide border security and would be available to protect the 134,000 Israeli settlers in these areas. The peace pact was put in place in 1994. Meanwhile, the long-standing dispute over who would control Jerusalem was still uncertain. Further negotiations for a permanent solution were scheduled for 1995. Still, the anger and hatred in the Middle East escalated again, and violence continued.

Swissair Disaster

On September 2, 1998, Swissair flight 111 crashed into the icy ocean off Peggy's Cove in Nova Scotia, Canada. All 229 people on board the jet were killed. The aircraft was flying out of John F. Kennedy Airport on its way to Geneva, Switzerland, when, nearly an hour into the flight, the crew noticed an odor in the cockpit. They thought it was a problem with the air-conditioning system. The smoke began to fill the cockpit, and the pilot contacted Canadian air-traffic controllers to let them know about the problem. Within a minute, the pilots were wearing oxygen masks, and they had declared an emergency. The controllers and crew decided to land the aircraft immediately at Halifax, Nova Scotia. They thought that they should dump fuel before landing, so they turned to do so over the water. The pilots turned off autopilot to fly manually. At 10:26 PM, Swissair flight 111 vanished from radar, and five minutes later, it crashed into the water.

Hong Kong to China Again

After a ninety-nine-year lease of Hong Kong, Britain returned it to Chinese control on July 1, 1997. Hong Kong's last British governor, Chris Patten, handed over the government, while worried citizens sat concerned about the future. Many feared that they would lose their democratic traditions now that they were under Chinese rule. The first pro-democracy demonstration filled Hong Kong's streets on the very day that rule was transferred. Other people worried about China's poor civil-rights record. Six hours after British troops withdrew from Hong Kong, Chinese tanks rolled in to replace them. Despite the change of ownership, Hong Kong continued to prosper as it had under British rule. The Chinese had promised "one country, two systems," meaning that Hong Kong would not be made communist like the rest of China. It would carry on as before, democratically.

■ On the first day of Chinese rule, about 3,000 pro-democracy protesters lined the streets of Hong Kong.

PEOPLE'S PRINCESS DEAD

■ On August 30, 1997, regular television programming around the world was interrupted to bring a tragic story to the public. Diana, Princess of Wales, had been in a car accident in Paris. The car she and friend Dodi Fayed were traveling in had been speeding down Paris streets in an attempt to escape **paparazzi**. The driver lost control and the car smashed into a tunnel. Diana and Fayed, as well as the chauffeur, died of their injuries. The princess's bodyguard was badly injured but survived the crash. The world was stunned that the woman who had brought so much good to the world was gone. Millions of people watched Diana's funeral on television or gathered in England to watch the procession. Grief and sympathy for Diana's family turned to anger at the relentless photographers and newspaper journalists who had chased her to her death.

Operation Desert Storm

On January 17, 1991, the U.S. declared war on Iraq. Operation Desert Storm, under the guidance of General Norman Schwarzkopf, immediately began bombing Baghdad. The state-of-the-art weapons and equipment included laser-guided "smart bombs." In the first few days, the U.S. and other allied countries launched thousands of raids against Iraq and Kuwait, which was occupied by Iraq. To fight back, Saddam Hussein ordered attacks on Israeli cities and on U.S. military bases in Saudi Arabia. On January 29, ground troops went into action. After three days of fighting, the U.S. troops pushed the Iraqis back, but suffered the loss of twelve Marines. In the end, U.S.

Soldiers survey the remnants of an Iraqi SCUD missile.

power proved too much for the ill-equipped Iraqi soldiers. Before retreating, Iraqis set fire to hundreds of Kuwait's oil wells. The next battle was to put out the blazes. By February 28, the war was over. Kuwait was an independent nation again, but its freedom came at a cost. In the short conflict, 148 U.S. troops were killed and 472 were wounded. Iraq suffered approximately 150,000 casualties. Thousands of Iraqis surrendered or gave themselves over to the allies. Despite riots and damage to the country, Hussein remained in charge. The Persian Gulf area was full of refugees, and much of it was polluted because of the burning oil wells.

Free at Last

In the mid-1980s, seventeen Americans were taken hostage in Lebanon. On December 4, 1991, the last of these hostages was released. Terry Anderson, the Associated Press bureau chief, had been a captive for 2,455 days—the longest period of any of the U.S. hostages. He had been taken at gunpoint by the terrorist group Islamic Jihad on March 16, 1985, while on his way home from playing tennis. During his captivity, Anderson was chained and blindfolded. He lived on bread, cheese, and water. Every day, as he was moved from cell to cell, he feared he would be killed. Others who had been kidnapped were killed or died—CIA Station Chief William Buckley, Marine Lt. Col. William R. Higgins, and librarian Peter Kilburn all lost their lives in Lebanon. Two of the bodies were left on the streets after Anderson's release so that they could be returned to their families for burial. Anderson's release followed that of fellow captives Alann Steen and Joseph Cicippio earlier that week. Upon returning home, Anderson filed a lawsuit against Iran for the kidnapping and was awarded more than $300 million. He wanted the terrorist country to pay for what it had done, but he doubted he would ever see the money. He asked President Clinton to use some of the hundreds of millions of dollars in frozen Iranian assets to pay the lawsuit, but the government was not eager to do so.

The Bush Years

President George Bush wanted to help American citizens. He passed the Americans with Disabilities Act in 1990. This Act made life easier for people who were physically or mentally challenged. It was one of the most comprehensive civil-rights laws of the nineties. Bush worked hard to improve education, childcare, and technological research and development. He wanted the U.S. to be the best country possible. Bush continued his crusade to get tough on crime by passing a bill to make it easier for police officers to bring criminals to justice. Bush then tried to make up for the lack of attention paid to

environmental problems in the past. Bush put higher standards of air quality in place with the Clean Air Act. This did what no other president had done for years—it brought business interests and environmental concerns together.

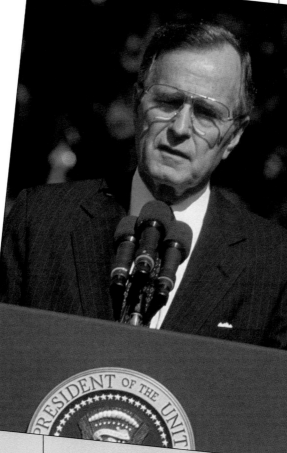

■ George Bush's social programs helped millions of Americans.

KEATING FIVE

■ On November 15, 1990, the Senate Ethics Committee held hearings about a group of senators called the Keating Five. These senators became involved with banking regulators on behalf of businessman Charles Keating, Jr. Keating was a savings and loan director who had given a great deal of money to the senators' campaigns. Keating had mismanaged money and committed fraud, costing taxpayers $2.6 billion. He and other corrupt executives created a banking failure in the late-1980s, which ended up costing taxpayers approximately $500 billion. This corruption and the five senators associated with it raised red flags with the ethics committee. The committee found California Senator Alan Cranston guilty of misconduct. The four other senators were less severely punished. Keating, on the other hand, was convicted of fraud, conspiracy, and racketeering, and was sentenced to more than twelve years in jail and fined $122.4 million.

Brady Bill

The number of gun-related deaths in the U.S. was staggering in the 1990s. This high level of violence caused people to rally for gun control. Some people called for licensing or waiting periods for purchasing a gun. Several states have put these strategies into law, but many people continued to fight for national laws. James Brady and his wife, Sarah, strongly supported gun control. Brady had suffered brain damage after being shot during the 1981 assassination attempt on President Reagan. In 1993, Brady won a seven-year fight to make licensing and waiting periods a part of law. The Brady Bill required a five-day waiting period to buy a gun. This allowed local officials to check the application to ensure the purchaser was qualified to own a handgun. The bill also created a $200 firearm license fee and a $90 annual renewal fee for guns. The efforts to control guns were praised. Still, responsible gun owners argued that they were paying the price, while people who were using their weapons to commit crimes would not register their guns and would simply buy weapons from other criminals on the street.

Bill Clinton President

American voters decided that they were ready for a change. They found that change with Democrat Bill Clinton. The 46-year-old politician was the first president born after World War II. He told Americans that he was a "New Democrat." He still believed in the traditional Democratic principles, but he also wanted to cooperate with business. People liked what they heard. In the 1992 election, he received 43 percent of the popular vote, while Bush received 38 percent.

Clinton had a clear vision of what he wanted to do. He promised to put Americans back to work and to reform the health-care system. The new president also looked beyond his country's borders and assured citizens that he would move ahead in trade and peace talks between Israel and its neighbors. He would also

■ Bill Clinton was the third-youngest U.S. president.

negotiate arms agreements with Russia, and he would help famine-stricken Somalia. Clinton's good looks and charm made him an extremely popular president, even in the face of personal scandals.

PEROT FOR CHANGE

■ In 1992, businessman H. Ross Perot ran as an independent candidate for the presidency. Many people in Washington, DC, did not think this Texan billionaire stood a chance, but they underestimated him. Perot's campaign focussed on problems in government programs—namely, a collapsing health-care system, huge **deficit** spending, corrupt financial practices during campaigns, and the growing gap between voters and politicians. Perot accused the parties of disregarding the needs of the American people and not moving forward on important issues.

Many Americans were surprised when Perot pulled ahead of President Bush and Bill Clinton in opinion polls. They were further surprised when he pulled out of the race in July because of the toll it was taking on his family. Perot re-entered the race in October, and to make up for lost time, he spent $37 million on television ads. This brought his total personal campaign spending to $60 million. In the election, Perot received 19 percent of the vote, the highest number an independent candidate had received since 1912.

"The Body" for Governor

Most Americans knew Jesse "The Body" Ventura as a popular professional wrestler. Others knew him as an actor who starred in many movies, including *Predator* with Arnold Schwarzenegger. In 1990, Ventura decided to run for mayor of Brooklyn Park in Minnesota. He thought the best way to protect the wetland was to be part of the legislative body making decisions about it. He was elected mayor and served until 1995. At that time, the ex-Navy SEAL broadened his ambitions. He decided to throw his hat into the state political ring and run for governor. He amazed people when he and his running mate, teacher Mae Schunk, beat Attorney General Hubert H. Humphrey III and St. Paul Mayor Norm Coleman at the polls in 1998. Ventura became the only Reform Party candidate to be elected to a statewide office. Ventura, the thirty-eighth governor of Minnesota, promised voters an efficient administration that followed common sense. He promoted education and worked toward improving the state's schools and decreasing class sizes. He also tried to bring in tax reforms. Ventura did not lose his love for sports or for the spotlight. In 2000, he became a commentator for the XFL football league.

Bad Press for the President

Attorney General Janet Reno launched an investigation into an Arkansas real estate company in 1994. Bill and Hillary Clinton, as well as James McDougal, had invested in this company, called Whitewater Development Corporation, in the 1970s. Regardless of the help, Whitewater lost money, and so did the Clintons. Their business partners bought a savings and loan association. There were rumors that Whitewater had bought land with the company's account at the savings and loan. That savings and loan group went bankrupt in 1989, and the federal bailout that followed cost taxpayers $60 million. An investigation into the failed savings and loan association was launched.

As a result, the president's involvement was investigated, and Hillary Clinton was called to testify before the grand jury. The committee wanted to find out about the connection between the Clintons and McDougal, whether

money from the savings and loan was put through Whitewater to pay for Clinton's campaign, and whether the Clintons received undue income tax benefits from the failure of Whitewater. The committee also wanted to investigate whether Clinton had used his position at the time—governor of Arkansas—to help the company. The investigations continued until 1997, and several people were found guilty of fraud and conspiracy. Although the committee could not prove any wrongdoing by the president, the constant publicity hurt his image and his ability to run his administration effectively.

■ James McDougal was convicted of fraud in the Whitewater scandal, and was sentenced to eighty-four years in prison. His sentence was later reduced to three years.

Shift of Power

In 1994, the congressional elections resulted in a shift in power in the Senate and House of Representatives. The Republicans now had a 52-48 majority in the Senate. Two more Democratic senators switched parties shortly after the election, upsetting the balance even more. The House of Representatives also enjoyed a 230-204 Republican majority. The president and the majority did not always see eye-to-eye. Many initiatives put forth by the Republican Congress were stopped by the president's **veto** or the threat of a veto. Clinton and the Republicans in Congress could not come to an agreement on the federal budget for 1996. They argued about how to cut spending and how to change the welfare system. The president argued against huge cuts in Medicare, Medicaid, education, and environmental projects. It took until April for the president and Congress to meet in the middle. They approved a budget that provided funds for government agencies until the end of October. This included the Republicans' cuts in spending to art, labor, and housing, but the budget also protected several of the education and environmental programs that Clinton wanted.

Beloved Author

Since the 1970s, Toni Morrison had been amazing critics and audiences with her soulful writing. She has won nearly every major literary prize in the country, including the National Book Critics' Circle Award, the National Book Foundation Medal for Distinguished Contribution to American Letters, and the Pearl S. Buck Award. Her 1987 novel, *Beloved*, earned her the Pulitzer Prize for fiction. It was also made into a motion picture starring Oprah Winfrey. Morrison explored the lives of troubled characters in her novels. She tried to help them find themselves and their culture in a society that did not value such discovery. Many of her novels brought the struggles of African Americans to light. In 1993, she was honored with a Nobel Prize for Literature for

■ Toni Morrison accepts her Nobel Prize in Stockholm, Sweden.

"Winning as an American is very special, but winning as a Black American is a knockout."

Toni Morrison on winning the 1993 Nobel Prize for Literature

her impressive body of work. She became the first African-American woman to be given this prestigious award. Her novels include *Song of Solomon*, *Tar Baby*, *Jazz*, and *The Bluest Eyes*.

WORLD FOCUS

MAGICAL STORY

An unknowing wizard captured the imagination of readers around the world in the nineties. Author J. K. Rowling's Harry Potter and the Philosopher's Stone *was published in Britain in 1997 and was an immediate success. It won the Smarties Book Prize gold medal for ages 9 to 11 and was named the British Book Awards' Children's Book of the Year. The U.S. rights were bought for $105,000—more than any other first-time children's author had received. At last, Rowling could quit her job and write full time.*

The book, renamed Harry Potter and the Sorcerer's Stone, *reached the U.S. in 1998 and topped both the children's and adult's bestseller lists. Readers of all ages were entranced by the young boy, his friends, and their adventures at Hogwarts School of Witchcraft and Wizardry.*

The second installment of the series hit stores in June 1999. Harry Potter and the Chamber of Secrets *was just as successful as the first book. In September,* Harry Potter and the Prisoner of Azkaban *was released. The three Potter books claimed the top three spots on the New York Times Bestseller List for months.*

Harry Potter books have been translated into thirty languages, and a movie about the series was set for 2001.

ROMANCING READERS

■ Danielle Steel knew what made a great romance novel. Her characters and plots offered more than fantasy to her millions of loyal readers. Her stories were frequently about glamorous, wealthy people with fame and skyrocketing careers. They also explored betrayals, finding the right person, and the family dynamic. Much of what Steel wrote had been drawn, to some extent, from her own experiences. By the end of the nineties, Steel had written fifty bestselling novels. Many of her stories were produced as television movies. They drew large numbers of viewers and were praised by critics. The television movie, *Jewels* won two Golden Globe nominations.

Steel was not restricted to racy romance novels and screenplays. She also wrote the "Max and Marth" series of books for young readers. Ten illustrated books helped children face issues such as stepparents, new siblings, going to school, and the death of family members.

Literary Lawyer

Throughout most of the 1980s, John Grisham worked long hours in a Mississippi law firm. He was also elected to the House of Representatives in the state. He spent his spare time on his hobby—writing. At the courthouse, he heard the testimony of a young rape victim, and the compelling story started his brain churning. He began to write a novel about what would have happened if the girl's father had killed the men who attacked her. Three years later, in 1988, Grisham finished his first novel, *A Time to Kill*. Many publishers rejected his work, but Wynwood Press finally bought it and ran 5,000 copies—a very small number of books. Grisham was not discouraged. He had already started pounding out his next novel. This one was about a young attorney who was hired on at a seemingly perfect law firm. Of course, not everything was as

■ John Grisham's novels continue to top bestseller lists around the world.

it seemed. *The Firm* appeared on the bestsellers list for forty-seven weeks and was made into a movie starring Tom Cruise. With the fame and recognition this brought, Grisham could finally write full time. He became the king of legal thrillers. Many of his books were bestsellers, including *The Pelican Brief* (1992), *The Client* (1993), and *The Street Lawyer* (1998). Several were made into successful Hollywood films. During the nineties, there were more than 60 million Grisham novels in print in twenty-nine languages.

THE DARK SIDE

Anne Rice has always been attracted to the dark side of life. She explored this side in her successful novels. Her novels showed her interest in history, religion, philosophy, and fascinating characters. This New Orleans resident drew inspiration from the open-minded beliefs of her city. She wrote her first novel in only five weeks in 1973.

It took three years before *Interview with a Vampire* was published. It received mixed reviews, but Hollywood knew a winner when it saw one. Paramount Studios bought the film rights for $150,000. This opened the door for Rice's books to hit the mainstream.

Rice completed a five-book series called the "Vampire Chronicles," a three-book series on the Mayfair Witches, and other individual novels. *The Witching Hour* (1990), *Tale of the Body Thief* (1992), and *Lasher* (1993) are a few of Rice's bestselling novels. Rice had a large number of dedicated fans, who waited eagerly for each new book. Her novels *Violin* (1997) and *Pandora* (1998) had avid Rice readers lined up at bookstores for blocks. Whether under her real name or her pen names, A. N. Roquelaure and Anne Rampling, Rice enjoyed great success with the dark, supernatural side of life.

Probing Jupiter

NASA began its *Galileo* Project in 1989. It was an unmanned mission to gather information about the planet Jupiter and its surroundings. With the launch of the space shuttle, *Atlantis*, the project was on its way. It had a probe set up to enter Jupiter's atmosphere and an orbiter that made the probe circle the planet. The probe photographed Jupiter, its moons, and radiation belts. On December 7, 1995, the *Galileo* probe reached Jupiter's atmosphere. For the first time, the planet's atmosphere was measured. The results of these tests allowed scientists to answer many questions that had been asked about the solar system's largest planet. The probe became a part of Jupiter's atmosphere and the orbiter continued to observe the planet and send data back to Earth.

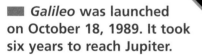 *Galileo* was launched on October 18, 1989. It took six years to reach Jupiter.

GENE THERAPY

■ Scientists had studied many gene diseases, but few were as awful as ADA deficiencies. This rare condition was caused by a defect in the gene that tells cells to produce adenosine deaminase—an enzyme that stops the buildup of toxins that can destroy the immune system. A drug was created to battle this disease in the eighties, but the expensive treatments did not always work. In September 1990, scientists made a breakthrough. A 4-year-old ADA sufferer became the first person to have her cells repaired or altered using one of the thousands of genes in DNA as a form of treatment. This successful gene therapy led to many experiments with other diseases, including cancer, AIDS, and cystic fibrosis.

WORLD FOCUS

INTERNET EXPLOSION

The U.S. National Science Foundation was the main financier of the worldwide computer grid called the Internet. The Internet had begun as a military system in 1969 and was used to link researchers' computers. Then it added libraries, universities, and other government departments. The military established 12,000 networks in forty-five countries. By 1993, 15 million people were using the Internet to research or chat with other "cybernauts." At this time, the foundation introduced a fast new system called T3. This system could handle 45 million bits of information per second. A revised T3 was soon operating at thirty times that speed. The communications capacity of this network grew enormously as the Internet spread throughout the world. More and more people became aware of "cyberspace" and the ability to use a personal computer to access information within seconds. With the Internet came instant messaging. E-mail became the preferred way to communicate with friends, family, and business associates, whether across the hall or across the world.

Lending a Hand

On January 24, 1999, a team of surgeons led by Dr. Jon Jones offered Matthew Scott a helping hand. They completed the first U.S. hand transplant. Scott had lost his left hand in a fireworks accident when he was 24 years old. Now, at the age of 38, he had a chance to make history and a new start. While surgeons had been reattaching severed limbs since the 1960s, they had never attached limbs from **cadavers** to living patients. This presented new obstacles and challenges. They had to prevent the patient's immune system from identifying the new limb as foreign and rejecting it. Using strong drugs, the surgeons were able to sidestep this problem. Within a year of the surgery, Scott was able to sense temperature, pressure, and pain with his new hand. He could also write, throw a baseball, and tie his shoelaces. The U.S. doctors were the second in the world to transplant a hand—the first hand transplant had occurred in France in 1998.

Biosphere Built

In October 1991, four men and four women took part in an incredible experiment. They started their two-year stay in a huge dome in the Arizona desert. A 3-acre sealed steel and glass enclosure was called Biosphere II. Inside Biosphere II were many miniature ecosystems, including a rain forest, a savanna, and an ocean. Also present were 3,800 species of plants and animals. The project was privately funded by Texas oil tycoon Edward Bass. He fronted the $150 million to get the project underway. Biosphere II was not as successful as everyone had hoped it would be. The crops within the enclosure failed, and in 1992, fresh air had to be pumped into the oxygen-starved dome. The eight residents abandoned the project in 1993.

The Eyes of Hubble

In 1990, decades of planning paid off. The *Hubble* telescope was finally put in orbit 370 miles above Earth. This $1.5 billion technological eye was sent into space to explore distant parts of the universe. NASA had high hopes for the telescope, but it was also faced with high costs. The telescope's mirror had been

■ The *Hubble* space telescope is as large as a school bus, weighs 12 tons, and has a mirror with an 8-foot diameter.

ground to the wrong curvature, which meant that blurry images were sent back to Earth. Within three years, three of *Hubble*'s **gyroscopes** had failed, and faulty solar panel supports trembled so badly in temperature changes that they could destroy the whole telescope at any moment. Despite these problems, the telescope managed to gather new information about the universe. For this reason, NASA decided to repair the mechanism. The shuttle *Discovery* blasted off in 1993, and crew members made the telescope as good as new. By then, the next generation of telescopes was beginning to appear. These new instruments gave more power and scope at a much lower cost.

Michael Jordan and the Bulls

In 1993, Michael Jordan shocked fans with his announcement that he would retire from basketball. At 30 years of age, the Chicago Bulls guard was the greatest player ever. He had claimed seven straight NBA scoring titles, three straight league Most Valuable Player awards, and two Olympic gold medals. He had led the team to six championship titles and averaged a record forty-one points per game in the finals in 1993. But this year had been difficult for the king of the court. His father was murdered in August, and the media swarmed with **allegations** of a gambling problem. Jordan decided to bow out of professional basketball and try his luck in baseball. A year and a half later, Jordan returned to the Bulls. Basketball fans welcomed him back with open arms. In 1996, Jordan received 2 million votes for the All-Star game, the most of any player ever. In all, he played in twelve All-Star Games and was the MVP of the game three times. That year, he also slam-dunked with Bugs Bunny and Tweety Bird in the hit movie *Space Jam*. Jordan again retired from the sport in 1998 as the Bulls' all-time leading scorer with 29,277 career points. He bought part of the Washington Wizards basketball team in 2000. Jordan fans held out hope that the man who could fly would return to the court again.

Tiger Woods

In 1997, a 21-year-old athlete amazed fans and other golfers. Tiger Woods earned his green jacket when he won the U.S. Masters tournament. He was the youngest person to win the tournament. While he was at it, he broke the all-time scoring record and won by the largest number of strokes. He finished 18 under par, with a total of 270 points and was twelve strokes ahead of his nearest opponent. He was also the youngest player to win the Grand Slam of professional golf championships—only five players have ever achieved this feat. Among Woods' other victories were the 2000 British Open, the 2000 U.S. Open, and the 1999 and 2000 Professional Golfers Association Championships. Often, Woods won these tournaments by record margins. In 1999, Woods won eleven worldwide championships. By then, he had twice been featured on the cover of *Sports Illustrated* as Sportsman of the Year, and he was named the Male Athlete of the Year by the Associated Press in 1997 and 1999, and was ESPY Male Athlete of the Year in 1997. In 1999, he was named World Sportsman of the Year by the World Sports Academy. On top of this, Woods was Player of the Year three times. With his mixed heritage of African American, Native American, Thai, and European, Woods was the first man of color to win a major professional golf championship. The ambitious golfer continued to win tournaments, endorse products, and set records into the twenty-first century.

■ Despite his young age, Tiger Woods is considered to be one of the best golfers ever.

Dream Team

In 1992, for the first time in Olympic history, professional basketball players were allowed to compete at the Games. The U.S. team put together probably the best team ever in Olympic competition. Team USA, dubbed the "Dream Team," boasted such superstars as Michael Jordan, Larry Bird, John Stockton, Magic Johnson, Charles Barkley, and Patrick Ewing. These players had been largely responsible for the skyrocketing popularity of basketball in the U.S. and throughout the world. This fast-

■ The Dream Team attracted fans and followers from around the world.

paced, exciting game was the fastest-growing sport in the U.S., and fans tuned in from home to watch their heroes playing together on the same team. The talented squad won all seven match-ups by an average of forty-four points and spent hours signing autographs for awestruck fans in Barcelona, Spain. They easily took home the gold medal. The Dream Team repeated this accomplishment at the 1996 Olympics in Atlanta, Georgia.

COMPETITIVE SPORT

■ In January 1994, athletes across the country were preparing for the Winter Olympic Games in Lillehammer, Norway. In figure skating, competition for medals was fierce even before the contenders left the U.S. Skater Tonya Harding tried to ensure her medal by eliminating her rival, Nancy Kerrigan. Harding's bodyguard hit Kerrigan on the knee with a metal bar after a practice for the Olympic trials. Harding hoped that the injury would leave Kerrigan unable to compete. Her ploy backfired. Kerrigan's injuries were not serious, and she recovered. It did not take long for Harding's part in the attack to surface. Harding became a sports villain. While she did not face criminal charges for her actions, she was kicked off the Olympic team. She successfully sued in order to remain a part of the U.S. figure-skating team. To the delight of many fans, Harding skated terribly in Lillehammer, while Kerrigan won a silver medal.

Yankees on Top

Between 1965 and 1994, the New York Yankees won only two World Series championships. Many people began to worry that the Yankees dynasty established by heroes such as Babe Ruth, Lou Gehrig, and Joe DiMaggio was over. In the mid-1990s, their fears were put to rest. A new wave of talented players hit Yankee Stadium like a shot. The team was back with a vengeance. Derek Jeter, Bernie Williams, and Paul O'Neill wowed baseball fans with their unstoppable hitting and unbreakable defense. The powerful pitching of Andy Pettitte and David Cone gave the Yankees the advantage they needed.

In 1996, the Yankees took home the World Series championship for the twenty-third time in history. After losing out on a repeat the following year, the Yankees reclaimed the trophy in 1998 with a sweep of the San Diego Padres and again in 1999 with a sweep of the Atlanta Braves. David Wells achieved a perfect game in 1998 and David Cone did so the following year—no opposing player reached first base. In 2000, the Yankees became the first team in more than twenty-five years to "three-peat" a World Series championship when they beat the New York Mets for the title.

Venus the Tops

Venus Williams made her professional tennis debut in 1994 at 14 years of age. At the Bank of the West Classic in Oakland, California, the young player nearly knocked the number-two player out of the tournament. Williams led the match but could not hold on to it. Her performance caught the attention of many people in the tennis world. Her 108-mph serve shocked fans in 1996—it was the ninth-fastest serve on the tour. Williams worked hard every day to claw her way from a 211th- to a 64th-place ranking in 1997, but she had not yet won a championship. She did not have to wait long. She continued to reach the semifinals in 1998 in such tournaments as the U.S. Open and the Australian Open. Then she won her first singles title—the IGA Tennis Classic. From there, she skyrocketed to the top. Her ranking shot

◼ Venus Williams learned to play tennis when she was 5 years old.

to number twelve in the world, and she beat established players, including Anna Kournikova, in an all-teen final. She then won the Grand Slam Cup and set a women's world record for her 127-mph serve at the Swisscom Challenge.

She and her sister, Serena, went on to make history together. In 2000, they were the first sisters ranked in the Top Ten at the same time since 1991, and

they were the first sisters to win a Grand Slam crown together in the twentieth century. Williams won a gold medal in singles competition at the 2000 Olympics, as well as a doubles gold medal with Serena. She also won the Wimbledon tournament. Williams and her flashy outfits brought more pizzazz to tennis and kept all eyes focused on her rise to stardom.

Road to Success

Lance Armstrong proved what it meant to be a champion. In 1991, the 20-year-old was the U.S. National Amateur Champion in road cycling, and he finished fourteenth at the Olympic Games in 1992. After that, he worked hard to compete professionally. He soon had countless titles under his belt, including the Motorola championships from 1992 to 1996, the World Championship in 1993, and the U.S. Championship in 1993.

For the next few years, Armstrong rode in Europe, often the only American in the running. He won the $1 million Thrift Drug Triple Crown and then the 1995 Tour Du Pont, earning the title of the Velo News American Male Cyclist of the Year.

In 1996, Armstrong hit a bump in the road—he was diagnosed with cancer. But he would not give up, and his spirit and medical treatment got him back on his feet. He returned to competition in 1998 with a win at the Sprint 56K Criterium. Armstrong proved he was better

than ever with victories at the Tour de Luxembourg in June and the Rheinland-Pfalz Rundfarht and the Cascade Classic in July. He finished fourth at the World Championships that year in horrible weather and racing conditions. Armstrong added an incredible chapter to his racing career in 1999. He finally won the **grueling** Tour de France. He repeated the performance the following year. Armstrong continued to be one of the most enthusiastic cycling competitors in the country into the twenty-first century.

Magic Johnson

Earvin Johnson was an undisputed favorite of Los Angeles Lakers fans. Throughout the 1980s, "Magic" Johnson had controlled the basketball court and was one of the best point guards and playmakers the game had ever known. In November 1991, he shocked the sporting world with his announcement that he was HIV-positive. He was going to retire from playing and intended to campaign for awareness about AIDS. Johnson became a spokesperson for AIDS awareness, and he created a foundation to promote research into the disease. In 1992,

■ Magic Johnson is one of the most vocal activists in the fight against HIV and AIDS.

he published the book, *What You Can Do to Avoid AIDS.* That year, Johnson returned to basketball at the NBA All-Star Game. After this appearance, the Lakers retired his jersey— number thirty-two. Johnson helped the Dream Team win the gold medal at the 1992 Olympic Games in Barcelona, Spain, all

the while serving on the President's Council on AIDS. Magic returned to professional basketball in September 1992, signing a contract with the Los Angeles Lakers. His return was short-lived. He announced his retirement when people started saying that he might spread the disease to other people. Magic did not stray far from the sport he loved. He became a television commentator and then the head coach of the Lakers for the 1993–94 season. Magic Johnson made one last return to basketball in 1996 as a Laker, but he retired for good after the team was beaten in the first round of the playoffs.

WRESTLEMANIA

■ In the 1990s, professional wrestling topped television ratings and attracted huge live crowds. People could not get enough of wrestlers Hulk Hogan, the Undertaker, Stone Cold Steve Austin, and Chyna. About 22 million people tuned in each week to watch the unfolding stories about their favorite wrestlers. While the matches were all predetermined, the performances were athletically and physically demanding. Wrestlers flew from the top ropes, performed complicated flips, and hit each other with garbage cans. All the while, fans cheered or booed enthusiastically, depending on who was in the ring. The World Wrestling Federation, or WWF, had about 125 performers on the payroll to fight for titles and to brawl backstage. In 1999, the company earned revenues of more than $250 million. By 2000, revenues had climbed to nearly $380 million. With pay-per-view specials, home videos, and weekly shows, the popularity of professional wrestling continued to soar.

Fans Shut Out

In 1994, baseball fans were informed that there would not be a World Series. The players were on strike, and there seemed no hope to end it. All but two team owners agreed to cancel the season. Peter Angelos, owner of the Baltimore Orioles, agreed with the spirit of the decision but wanted it worded differently to explain his position better. Cincinnatti Reds owner Marge Schott, who had been the center of **controversy** before, wanted to continue the season with replacement players. She wanted to watch "real" players, not the "million-dollar babies" who had been playing the game. The strike carried on for 234 days. On April 2, 1995, the two sides finally reached an agreement. The 1995 season kicked off, but not all was forgiven. Fans were angry at the strike and were slow to support their home teams.

The Juice on Trial

Before 1994, O. J. Simpson was known as a football hero, an actor, and a product **pitchman**. On June 13, 1994, everything changed. His ex-wife, Nicole Brown Simpson, and her friend Ronald Goldman, were found brutally murdered at her townhouse in Los Angeles. Simpson was the immediate suspect. The police planned to arrest him when Simpson took off in his Ford Bronco, leading a slow-speed highway chase. Millions of people watched the chase on television and speculated about his innocence or guilt. He eventually surrendered to police but insisted he was innocent.

The trial that followed in January 1995 was a circus. It was televised, which caused lawyers, witnesses, and even the judge to perform a bit more than they should in a court of law. Talk show and news program hosts discussed the day's events, feeding society's appetite for more about the Simpson trial.

The trial explored issues of race relations, police procedures, and domestic violence, all the while dividing the nation. In October, the trial was finally over and the jury acquitted "The Juice." The families of both victims were enraged. A civil trial in 1997 found Simpson responsible of the victims' deaths, and he was ordered to pay millions of dollars to their families. The debate over Simpson's guilt or innocence continued long after the trial had ended.

ECONOMY DOWN

■ In 1990, a mild recession hit the U.S. It lasted only six months, but people felt its impact for much longer. The government increased spending on welfare and other social programs, causing more strain on the country's pocketbook. The situation improved slightly, but the economy did not flourish.

By January 1992, unemployment levels were the highest they had been since 1987. In the country, 7.1 percent of the employable population was looking for work. Then IBM announced a loss of $564 million for 1991—the first time in the company's history that it lost money. At the end of January, TWA sunk to bankruptcy with a $2 billion debt. In February, General Motors announced its most significant loss in its history, with a $4.5 billion hit. Ford also posted record losses with $2.3 billion. Americans struggled through the tough economic times of the early- to mid-nineties to enjoy sunnier days later in the decade.

Million Man March

In October 1995, hundreds of thousands of African-American men gathered in Washington, DC, to make their voices heard. The rally was organized to encourage African-American men to confirm their dedication to their families, communities, education, and personal responsibilities. Louis Farrakhan, leader of the religious group Nation of Islam, was the man behind the march. He followed some beliefs of Islam, but he also believed in African-

■ More than 800,000 people attended the march in Washington, DC.

American self-sufficiency. Farrakhan's views against Jewish people and his push to separate the races alienated many African Americans, and some leaders refused to take part in the march. Many others who marched said that they did not support all of Farrakhan's opinions, but they felt it was important to come together at the demonstration.

While Farrakhan did not get the million people he hoped for, the march was viewed as a success. It was a peaceful demonstration that required a great deal of planning on the part of the city. Officials needed to find somewhere to park the 11,000 buses used to carry marchers to Washington. They tried to find 3,000 portable toilets for the huge number of people, and streets around the Capitol had to be closed. Police officers were on hand, just in case, but they were not needed.

■ The Rodney King incident inspired a number of protests calling for justice.

Video Causes Riots

On March 3, 1991, Los Angeles police officers chased a car whose driver would not pull over. When it stopped, police pulled a 25-year-old African American, Rodney King, from the vehicle and began to beat him. They claimed he had not followed instructions to lie flat. King received fifty-six baton blows and six kicks, which caused brain and kidney damage and eleven skull fractures. The attack was caught on video by a man on a nearby balcony. By the end of the next day, the recording of four police officers clubbing King, who was lying on the ground, was featured on every news program in the country. Four officers were charged with using **excessive** force and assault with a deadly weapon. Officers Stacey Koon (the supervisor), Larry Powell, Theodore Briseno, and Timothy Wind all pleaded not guilty.

> "I just couldn't understand why they were continuing what I saw there was no reason for."
>
> Officer Briseno, on why he tried to push Powell away from King

The officers' trial began a year later. It was moved to the suburb of Simi Valley to guarantee the defendants a fair trial. On April 29, 1992, the men were acquitted. Areas where African Americans lived erupted in violence. The streets of Los Angeles were filled with rioters. Federal troops tried to calm the situation. In six days, 54 people were killed, 2,383 were injured, and 13,212 people were arrested. The rioting caused about $700 million in property damage. On May 2, the U.S. Justice Department announced that it would investigate the officers on civil rights violations. Racial conflicts continued throughout the summer until the officers were **arraigned** on federal charges on August 5, 1992. On April 17, 1993, Koon and Powell were found guilty and sentenced to thirty months in prison.

The Curse of Camelot

Many people thought that the Kennedy family was cursed. It had endured tragic deaths and scandals for decades. Joseph Kennedy, Jr., had died in a plane crash at the age of 29, as had Kathleen Kennedy at the age of 28. The assassinations of Robert and John Kennedy in the sixties reaffirmed the belief in a family curse.

In January 1998, Michael, son of Robert Kennedy, was skiing in Aspen, Colorado. He hit a tree head-first and died about an hour later. Michael had been in the media because of a scandal, the other part of the Camelot Curse. His affair with a babysitter had embarrassed the family and caused his older brother, Joseph, to withdraw from the governor's race in Massachusetts.

The family had barely recovered from Michael's death when John, Jr., was killed in an airplane crash in July 1999. He was flying to a wedding with his wife, Carolyn Bessette, and her sister Lauren. Kennedy was a fairly inexperienced pilot flying a complicated plane. The plane crashed in fog and was found off Martha's Vineyard. The bodies were recovered a few days later. John, Jr., was adored by Americans, and his death was a blow to the country.

In 1990, President Bush had the task of breathing life into a failing economy. The federal budget deficit had soared to $220 billion per year, which was three times what it was in 1980. The debt had swelled to $3.2 trillion, which was also three times that of 1980. The president tried to find common ground between the Democrats and the Republicans in Congress in order to establish a way to pay down the debt. Many Democrats thought that increasing taxes for wealthy people was the best solution. Republicans disagreed. They felt that federal spending cuts were the only way to cure the deficit problem.

Congressional Democrats told Bush that he had to sign a statement calling for tax revenue increases before there were any further discussions about the budget. Bush did not think this would go against his campaign promise of no new taxes. He was wrong. Republican supporters were angry. They pulled their support for the president and defeated the budget bill in the House of Representatives.

■ **Demonstrators with the Philadelphia Unemployment Project rally on the steps of the U.S. Capitol.**

Downsizing

The word "downsizing" was used in the 1970s to refer to smaller homes and cars that people chose in order to combat high energy prices. By the 1990s, the term referred to people. Between 1992 and 1997, 16.4 million Americans were victims of downsizing. At the same time, companies' profits and stock values rose. The heads of major corporations made higher salaries than CEOs anywhere else in the world, even when profits were stable or dropping. The message was clear: cutting jobs was a way to get ahead in business.

Companies replaced their high-salaried American workers with those willing to work for much less and in countries with looser environmental and labor rules.

While downsizing may have increased the bottom line, it did not necessarily make for an efficient workplace. People did not feel secure in their jobs. They knew they could be let go at any time, even if they were doing good work. The challenges and hardships associated with downsizing stayed with U.S. workers and families well past the nineties.

Free Trade

President Bush wanted to boost U.S. trade. He suggested a North American Free Trade Agreement (NAFTA) as a way to do this. An agreement with Mexico and Canada would reduce or even remove trade **tariffs** on goods sold across the continent. Both Canada and Mexico were interested in the agreement and saw it as a way of helping North America compete with such areas as Asia and Europe, which already had free-trade zones. Bush's successor, Bill Clinton, carried on the agreement with Canadian Prime Minister Brian Mulroney and Mexican President Carlos Salinas de Gortari.

NAFTA was passed by Congress in 1993 after a great deal of debate. It was put into effect in 1994. Many Americans and Canadians were afraid that companies would move their factories to Mexico to save money and that jobs would be lost as a result. Others were concerned that environmental regulations would be harder to enforce under NAFTA. Some of the concerns raised were dealt with in additional agreements in 1993 before NAFTA was approved.

■ Electrical Workers Union President William Bywater makes a speech protesting NAFTA.

MINIMUM WAGE

■ In April 1990, the minimum wage for U.S. workers rose to $3.80. It increased again in 1991 to $4.25. Critics said that the increase would cause financial problems for small businesses, which would not be able to afford the higher wages. They claimed that it might cause people to lose their jobs. Despite these concerns, the minimum wage was raised to reflect **inflation** and the cost of living. However, the government recognized the concerns and said there could be a lower wage for training workers. These workers, who were often between the ages of 16 and 19, earned $3.61 per hour. This training wage would expire on March 31, 1993.

Balancing Act

President Clinton was dedicated to balancing the federal budget. With this promise came tax cuts for millions of people. The plan to balance the budget was the first of its kind since 1969. It stated that the federal deficit could be scrapped by 2002 if the U.S. economy stayed strong. A balanced budget came with a price. Clinton's bill called for government cuts. He expected to trim federal spending by $263 billion over five years. This included removing $140 billion from the government's compulsory programs, such as Medicare and Medicaid—the health programs for poor and elderly Americans. His bill also introduced $24 billion in new funding that would give uninsured children health coverage. Clinton left office before seeing if his plan would be a success.

Grunge Gives Way to Glamour

In the 1990s, America was introduced to "grunge." This style came alongside a new type of music from Seattle, Washington. Nirvana, Pearl Jam, and Soundgarden were some of the grunge bands that made the new sound popular. Fans began dressing in large flannel work shirts worn over T-shirts and baggy, ripped jeans. Comfort was the key, and looking sloppy was a bonus. Considering fans spent a great deal of time "moshing" to the alternative band's music, this focus on comfort made sense.

Toward the end of the nineties, people began growing out of grunge. They wanted something a bit more stylish. Glamour was the order of the day. This, too, went along with a music style. Rather than hard rock, swing and jazz bands gained popularity in the U.S. This brought a renewed interest in the styles of the 1920s and 1930s. Women began wearing cocktail dresses out on the town, finishing off the glamorous look with gloves. Men donned linen suits, hats, and wing-tipped shoes when heading out for the evening. The late-nineties looked like a scene out of history—people danced the jitterbug, sipped fancy drinks, and were dressed to the nines.

Friendly Fashions

The huge success of the sitcom *Friends* did more than boost network ratings. It influenced the way Americans dressed and styled their hair. Salons from coast to coast were swamped with women wanting the shaggy, layered look of "Rachel" or the shorter bob often worn by "Monica" on the show. "Phoebe" introduced women to sassy hair clips and accessories. Actresses had not caused such a fashion stir since Farrah Fawcett's feathered locks in the 1970s. As the seasons passed, the actresses changed their hairstyles, and U.S. women changed along with them. U.S. men also got in on the *Friends*

■ The cast of *Friends,* with their trendy and sophisticated styles, influenced fashion around the globe.

frenzy. The brushed-forward style worn by "Joey" and the spiky look that "Ross" sported found their way into U.S. salons. The six stars continued to lead the fashion brigade throughout the decade.

Seventies Revival

Disco found its way back during the 1990s, at least as far as fashion was concerned. Young people relived a decade they had not even been around to experience the first time. Polyester shirts, of both solid colors and patterns, flew off store racks. Flared jeans, or bell bottoms, were on every teenager's wish list. Many styles had flowers printed or embroidered onto pockets or pant legs. Short shorts, called hot pants, worn with halter tops also returned to women's wardrobes. The seventies revival would not be complete without platform shoes. Girls and women were suddenly three or four inches taller in this footwear. The shoes caused some problems, though. British pop star Baby Spice fell while wearing platform shoes. So did many others.

■ The revival of 1970s fashions renewed an interest in second-hand clothing stores.

The colors and accessories of the nineties also smacked of the 1970s. Hot pink, burnt orange, and powder blue all came back into fashion. Brown polyester was the choice fabric for pantsuits, jackets, and shirts.

To add something extra to these recycled styles, many designers added sequins and glitz. Americans loved this glance to the past and added powder blue eye shadow to make the look authentic.

LABEL CRAZY

■ Fashionable Americans in the 1990s were influenced by brand names. Tommy Hilfiger, Nautica, and GAP were labels that all stylish people needed to have on their clothes. These names were not only on the inside label—they were often splashed across the front of shirts. Designers and stores supported the casual trend of clothing. GAP stores were lined with row upon row of T-shirts and sweatshirts, along with khaki skirts and cargo pants.

Tommy Hilfiger fashions, which could be found in large department stores, dressed men and women in upper crust style. The brand names were also attached to popular perfumes and colognes. To dress the part was not enough—Americans had to smell the part as well.

Hip-Hop

Rap musicians had a style all their own in the nineties. Early in the decade, many of these rap stars wore tight-fitting knit caps, chunky jewelry, and expensive brand-name running shoes. Soon, fans began to adopt this way of dressing. U.S. youths began to wear blue jeans that were several sizes too big and hung below the waist. Hooded sweatshirts and baggy shorts were also rap-inspired inner-city fashions. Baseball caps were a must, but they were not worn traditionally. They were cocked to the side or worn backwards. Some hip-hop fans strung chains from their belt loops into their pockets, and the chain was attached to their wallets. Topping off the hip-hop look was a large jacket with a sport team's logo emblazoned on the back. The Los Angeles Raiders were favorite logos to wear on hats and jackets. Even young people who had not listened to the music borrowed some of the styles. Hip-hop or rap musicians continued to influence U.S. fashion throughout the nineties.

To USA or Bust

Cubans were taking their chances in leaky boats, rafts, and even inner tubes in order to become Americans. In the first half of 1994, thirteen boats were hijacked by Cubans who wanted to immigrate to the U.S. Several aircraft, including an airliner and a military helicopter, were also hijacked. Cuban leader Fidel Castro decided to let people leave if they wanted to. He announced that he would no longer stop them. Tens of thousands of Cubans rushed to Cuba's northwestern coast looking for ways to get to America. In August and early September, the U.S. Coast Guard **intercepted** more than 30,000 people on homemade rafts trying to reach America. Many empty rafts were found, which suggested that thousands of others had not survived the trip.

The rush of hopeful immigrants worried President

Clinton. Previously, the U.S. had automatically granted **asylum** to Cubans leaving the oppression of their home country. Clinton announced that this would no longer be the case. Instead, these people would be given safety at the U.S. Naval Base at Guantánamo Bay, Cuba. There, the "balseros," or boat people, would have to support their claims in order to become U.S. citizens. This did not slow the flow of refugees. On September 9, 1994, Clinton and Castro came to an agreement. Castro agreed

■ **Countless Cubans have risked their lives in hopes of finding freedom in the U.S.**

to try to prevent unsafe departures, and Clinton agreed to approve 20,000 visas per year for Cuban migrants. Also, any refugee who arrived in the U.S. would be the responsibility of relatives already in America. Those intercepted by the U.S. Coast Guard would be immediately returned to Cuba. Both sides hoped that this would calm the crisis.

Immigration Legislation

On September 25, 1996, the House of Representatives passed a new immigration bill. Its aim was to stop people from entering the U.S. illegally. To prevent **aliens** from sneaking across the border, the number of border patrol agents was increased to almost 10,000.

The bill also called for a 14-mile-long triple fence to be built along the U.S.-Mexican border near San Diego, California. Penalties for smuggling illegal immigrants into the U.S. or for using false documents to enter were increased. The immigration bill also made it more difficult for legal immigrants to receive welfare benefits. An August 1996 law excluded non-U.S. citizens from Food Stamp

assistance and Supplemental Security Income, and each state had to decide whether to allow legal immigrants to be part of the Medicaid program. President Clinton dropped some of the provisions of the bill, including one that would have allowed immigrants to be **deported** if they received welfare assistance for more than one year during their first seven years as U.S. citizens.

Caribbean Americans

Many changes to immigration policies occurred in the 1990s. Hondurans and Nicaraguans who had arrived in the U.S. by the end of 1998 were given the option to apply for Temporary Protected Status. This would allow them to stay in the U.S. until July 2000. In November 1998, the Immigration and Naturalization Service (INS) proposed the Nicaraguan Adjustment and Central American Relief Act. This required that Salvadorans and Guatemalans in the country by 1990 prove that they would experience "extreme hardship" if they were deported. In May 1999, the organization concluded that these people would, indeed, face extreme hardships if they returned to their countries of origin. The regulation would make most of the Central Americans and Eastern Europeans who requested asylum before 1992 eligible for immigrant status.

Welcome to America

In the mid-1990s, immigration exploded in the U.S. About 8 million people were eligible to apply for citizenship. Until 1994, only about 300,000 people per year did so. By 1995, the INS was processing about 1 million requests per year. That was about double the number in 1994. The number of applicants also continued to climb. In San Francisco, the INS launched a "Citizenship USA" campaign in May 1996. Los Angeles, Chicago, and Miami had hosted similar citizenship drives. The campaign aimed to swear in

■ On May 14, 1996, 1,700 new citizens take part in a mass ceremony in San Francisco, California.

1 million people by September. During the first quarter of 1996, San Francisco had 116,314 citizenship applications to process. This was a 53 percent increase from the same time the year before. That city alone hoped to swear in 18,000 new citizens per month. Other cities hosted enormous naturalization ceremonies. Irving, Texas, was one of them. In a mass naturalization ceremony at Texas Stadium on September 17, 1996, 10,000 newcomers swore their allegiance to the U.S. People

NEW HOME

■ Many people from all over the world came to the U.S. to start new lives. The chart below shows where some of these newcomers came from and how many new citizens arrived from these areas between 1991 and 1997:

Mexico	1,800,800
Philippines	401,900
South America	398,500
Central America	387,600
Former Soviet Union	377,700
China	303,400
Africa	245,900

were granted citizenship at an even larger ceremony of 11,000 in San Jose, California, the following day.

Many people felt that the dramatic increase in naturalization was due to anti-immigration laws and Americans' dislike of foreigners. Immigrants wanted to become citizens while they still could. Others thought that President Clinton was trying to create a large number of Democratic voters for the next election. The new Americans were encouraged to vote in elections.

FANTASTIC FESTIVALS

■ After attending a rock festival in England in 1990, Perry Farrell and Marc Geiger decided to repeat the experience in the U.S. They organized the first Lollapalooza festival in 1991. The tour began at the Shoreline Amphitheater south of San Francisco and traveled across the country, bringing alternative rock to eager fans. The Red Hot Chili Peppers, Ministry, and Pearl Jam were among the headliners. The shows averaged 11,000 screaming fans and were hugely successful. They organized festival after festival, headlining different bands each year. Some of those involved in Lollapalooza were Smashing Pumpkins, Jane's Addiction, and Nine Inch Nails. In 1998, the organizers could not find a headliner to draw the crowds needed, so the festival folded.

At the same time, a different kind of festival was enjoying rave reviews. Lilith Fair was a collection of female artists who toured Canada and the U.S. Sarah McLachlan organized the festival. It was the most successful festival of the year, drawing an average of 15,000 fans to each sold-out show. During the festival's three-year run, such stars as Bonnie Raitt, Jewel, Paula Cole, Sinéad O'Connor, and Sheryl Crow appeared on stage. Other lesser-known female singers and musicians were also able to get exposure and experience, thanks to Lilith Fair.

Top of the Hill

"Music is so important to me and how I come across in music is so important. I'm a perfectionist. If I have to do it a hundred times, I'll do it a hundred times."

Lauryn Hill on producing her own album

The rhythm and blues group the Fugees was incredibly successful in the 1990s. The group's album *The Score* sold more than 17 million copies and made the Fugees the bestselling rap group ever. Lauryn Hill's hauntingly beautiful voice was a big part of the group's success. Her version of "Killing Me Softly" became the hip-hop song of the decade. In 1998, she proved she was more than just a member of the Fugees. The music industry had been waiting for a solo album from Lauryn Hill, and *The Miseducation of Lauryn Hill* was worth the wait. The 23-year-old singer's album

■ *The Miseducation of Lauryn Hill* was the fastest-selling debut album for a female artist.

was full of songs that crossed genres—from hip-hop to Caribbean sounds. Hill's hard work was well rewarded. She won awards for her videos, as well as three Soul Train awards, and four NAACP awards. She was named the Favorite New Soul/R&B Artist at the American Music Awards in 1999. Hill boasted a record five Grammy Awards—for Album of the Year, Best New Artist, Best R&B Song, Best R&B Album, and Best Female R&B Vocal Performance.

Teen Pop

The music industry was overtaken by talented young stars in the late 1990s. "Boy bands," including *NSYNC and the Backstreet Boys, had teens buying albums in droves. The five handsome singers known as *NSYNC—Lance, J. C., Joey, Chris, and Justin—released their first album in 1998, selling more than 10 million copies and producing four number-one hits. Their next album, *No Strings Attached*, launched them to superstardom. The Backstreet Boys (BSB) followed a similar rise to the top. In 1993, Nick, A. J., Howie D., Brian, and Kevin enjoyed huge fame in Europe. They released their album in the U.S. in 1997, and it was a hit. In 1999, their album, *Millennium*, soared to the top of the charts. Both BSB albums were certified Diamond with 10 million sales each. That year, the group was nominated for five Grammy Awards, including one for Album of the Year.

Young men were not the only chart-toppers. Britney Spears sang and danced her way to the top as well. After appearing off-Broadway at 10 years of age and then on the *Mickey Mouse Club* television show, Spears began working with an agent to produce a record. In 1998, she finished her debut record and promoted it at malls. She also opened for *NSYNC in 1999 before the record hit store shelves. The 17-year-old bombshell's album reached number one. Her second album, *Oops!...I Did it Again*, sold 1.3 million copies during its first week. Although some parents criticized her for her racy outfits, Spears was a role model. Teen girls from coast to coast wanted to sing, dance, and be like her.

■ Before achieving stardom in the U.S., *NSYNC made their mark in Europe.

WORLD FOCUS

THREE TENORS

Opera fanatics worldwide were greeted with the concert of a lifetime during the 1990 World Cup soccer finals in Rome. The world's three top tenors, conducted by Zubin Mehta, entertained the 6,000-person crowd, while another 1.5 billion people watched on television. Spain's José Carreras and Placido Domingo, along with Italian opera hero Luciano Pavarotti, sang a program of familiar opera songs. The concert was such a hit that a video of the performance was released. The Three Tenors knocked Madonna out of the top spot in Great Britain. In the U.S., the tenors' opera album from that night reached number forty-three on the pop charts—the highest rank for a classical recording since the 1960s.

"When I was growing up, there were thirty great tenors, not three. I don't know why things are now the way they are."

Luciano Pavarotti

It also won a Grammy Award in 1991. In 1994, the tenors came together again for a recorded concert at Dodger Stadium in Los Angeles. The Three Tenors' albums became some of the bestselling classical records in history.

Clinton in Yugoslavia

After the breakup of Yugoslavia, the nation of Bosnia-Herzegovina was formed. A civil war in the area posed challenges for President Clinton. Bosnian Serb soldiers were better equipped than the Bosnian Muslims were, and they captured more land. President Clinton proposed bombing Serb supply lines and getting rid of an embargo that prevented weapons from reaching the Muslims. No other European country would support his proposals. In 1994, the president continued to pressure European leaders

■ **The Dayton Peace Agreement was intended to end fighting in the former Yugoslavia.**

to take action against the Serbs. In November, it seemed that the Serbs were about to take over Bosnian strongholds, so Clinton changed his mind. He decided to push for a settlement between the two sides.

In 1995, Clinton hosted peace negotiations between Bosnia and Herzegovina. The Dayton peace accord resulted. This kept the country whole but as two separated areas. In addition, Clinton promised to send U.S. soldiers to Bosnia and Herzegovina to assist NATO forces in providing aid and policing the area.

Americans in the Middle East

President Bush would not sit by and watch Iraq invade Kuwait in 1991. Within hours, he had contacted European, Asian, and Middle Eastern allies to help him stop Saddam Hussein. He even persuaded Saudi Arabia, which did not often allow foreign troops in its country, to allow U.S. soldiers to enter. Bush ordered the largest number of soldiers and supplies since the Vietnam War be sent to the Middle East.

In January 1991, the U.S. Congress approved Bush's proposal for military action, and the U.S. and its allies invaded Kuwait. The air and ground battles lasted until February. When the war was over, Bush had reached his goal—he had limited U.S. casualties and had returned Kuwait to its own government's control.

DEMOCRACY IN HAITI

■ American soldiers peacefully took over Haiti, an island in the Caribbean Sea, on September 19, 1994. The action started three years before when a military coup had taken over leadership from the country's first elected president, Jean-Bertrand Aristide. In 1993, President Clinton negotiated with the Haitian dictators in hopes of returning the former president. As part of the deal, the U.S. and the UN would help retrain the

country's military and police forces. When the time came, the dictators went back on the deal. Anti-Aristide protestors blocked American and Canadian ships from reaching the docks, so they turned back. Clinton insisted that the regime step down and restore democracy and the elected president. The military government ignored the warnings. In 1994, a large American force entered Haiti. Clinton sent former president Jimmy Carter to speak to the

military leader, Raoul Cédras, and persuade him to return control of the government and leave the country. Cédras finally agreed and handed back rule to Aristide. On October 13, Cédras and his lieutenants left Haiti and two days later the Americans brought Aristide home. Democracy was restored but troops remained to smoothen the transition. American troops pulled out in 1995 and UN troops remained until December 1997.

African Aid

In his final weeks as president in 1994, George Bush sent U.S. soldiers to the East African country of Somalia. Somalis were starving to death while trying to survive a brutal civil war. The U.S. troops were to make sure that food and other supplies reached the people. Local armed groups in the dispute turned their fire on Americans, and many people at home questioned their soldiers' involvement. When Clinton took over as president, he realized the seriousness of the situation. Rather than pulling troops out, he doubled efforts to make sure that the U.S. forces could defend themselves and fulfill their mission. That did not sit well with citizens in the U.S. They demanded that the soldiers return home. In March 1994, U.S. troops left Somalia, and UN troops took over their work.

U.S. involvement in Africa in the 1990s was not over. A civil war in Rwanda in 1994 caused millions of people to flee. Disease and starvation claimed many lives in refugee camps in neighboring countries. President Clinton sent food and supplies to the refugees in July. He also sent 200 soldiers to the capital city, Kigali, to make sure the relief supplies were delivered safely. The soldiers helped in the area until October.

After all the relations with Africa, the Clintons decided to make a six-nation tour to the continent in 1998. It was the most extensive visit to Africa by a U.S. president and the first time a U.S. president had visited South Africa. Clinton hoped to promote trade and investment while highlighting the success stories in Africa.

■ U.S. troops risked their lives to ensure that Somalis received basic necessities. Aid packages arrived from around the world.

BEING NEIGHBORLY

■ In 1995, the Mexican currency dropped quickly and many people feared that the country's economy would collapse. If that happened, the U.S. economy would suffer as well. President Clinton, together with Congress, tried to find a way to lessen the Mexican crisis. Congress refused to pass Clinton's plan to offer aid to Mexico. It did not think Americans would support this. Clinton did not give up. He created a $20 billion loan agreement with Mexico. The money would ease the anxiety of investors worldwide. This helped the Mexican economy recover. In January 1997, Mexico finished paying back the loan to the U.S. It had done so three years ahead of schedule.

A strong relationship with the U.S.'s southern neighbors was also apparent in 1996. Mexico and the U.S. joined forces in the war on drugs. Some members of Congress did not think that Mexico was doing enough to stop the illegal drug trade. In 1997, a top Mexican official was arrested for protecting a drug trafficker. Despite this, Clinton maintained the partnership to put an end to the illegal drug trade. He visited Mexico in May 1997, but the controversy, along with conflict about U.S. immigration policies, created tension between the two countries.

Where Did It Happen?

A Site of a school shooting

B Anne Rice's inspiration city

C Michael Jordan's home city

D Location of the Million Man March

E Where Jesse Ventura was mayor

F Magic Johnson coached this city's NBA team

G Site of Kennedy plane crash

H Originating city of grunge

I Where Lollapalooza began

J Site of a compound standoff

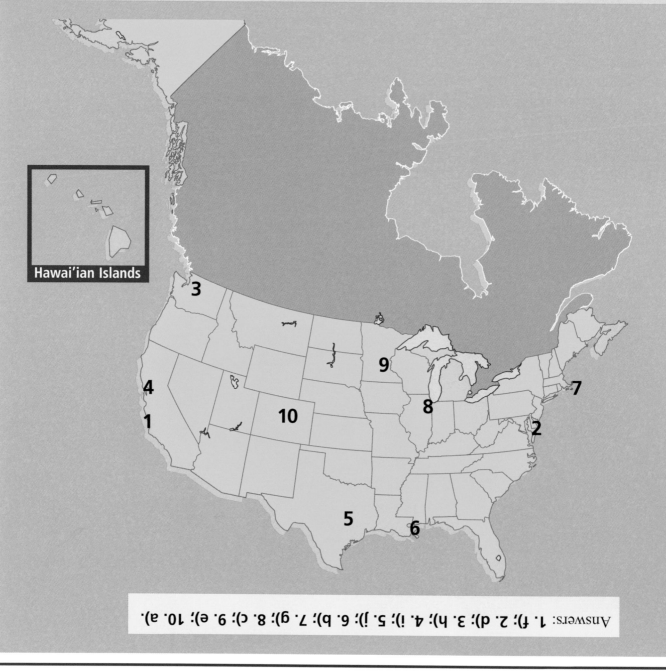

Hawai'ian Islands

Answers: 1. f); 2. d); 3. h); 4. i); 5. j); 6. b); 7. g); 8. c); 9. e); 10. a).

Choose the correct answer from the choices below.

1 "Balseros" were:
a) a popular swing band.
b) Cuban immigrants.
c) Hot new fashion for teens.

2 "Grunge" was:
a) a kind of music and fashion style.
b) nickname for a Green Bay Packers linebacker.
c) a code name for a Middle East operation.

3 Free trade:
a) cut sales taxes in forty-six states.
b) cut tariffs on international imports and exports.
c) increased tariffs on international imports.

4 ADA was:
a) an attention disorder scientists studied in the nineties.
b) an enzyme that stopped the buildup of toxins that destroyed the immune system.
c) an enzyme that promoted hair growth.

5 Venus Williams:
a) is a new star discovered by the *Hubble* telescope.
b) set a record for the fastest serve in tennis.
c) won a Pulitzer Prize for Literature.

Answers:
1. b); 2. a); 3. b); 4. b); 5. b).

Newsmakers

Match the names with their claim to nineties fame:

1. Grammy Award-winning hip-hop artist
2. ran for the presidency as an independent
3. Nobel Prize-winning author
4. involved in Whitewater scandal
5. Oscar-winning actress
6. gun-law activist
7. Israeli peacemaker
8. hostage in Lebanon
9. leader of the Branch Davidians
10. golf star

a) David Koresh
b) Terry Anderson
c) Julia Roberts
d) Yitzhak Rabin
e) Tiger Woods
f) Toni Morrison
g) Lauryn Hill
h) James Brady
i) James McDougal
j) Ross Perot

Answers: 1. g); 2. j); 3. f); 4. i); 5. c); 6. h); 7. d); 8. b); 9. a); 10. e).

aliens: people who are not legally allowed to be in a particular country

allegations: accusations

apartheid: the former system of separation of different races in South Africa

arraigned: called before a court

asylum: protection; place of safety

cadavers: corpses

controversy: dispute

coup: the overthrowing of a government by force

deficit: the amount of money spent over the amount of money earned

deported: removed from a country and sent back to one's country of origin

downsizing: reducing the number of employees

excessive: too much

grueling: very difficult and exhausting

gyroscopes: devices using heavy wheels that, when spinning quickly, hold direction

hard-line: strict

inflation: increase in prices and fall of the value of money

intercepted: stopped someone

naturalization: granting citizenship to people

paparazzi: photographers who pursue celebrities to take their picture

pitchman: someone who endorses a product or service

probe: a device used for space exploraion

prequel: the earlier part of a story

propaganda: spreading information that is exaggerated or untrue

sanctions: actions taken by a country against another to penalize it or cause it to follow the laws

tariffs: charges on imports and exports

terrorism: use of violence and intimidation, often for political purposes

veto: to reject or block a proposal

USA 1990s Learning More

Here are some book resources and Internet links if you want to learn more about the people, places, and events that made headlines during the 1990s.

Books

Boyd, Aaron. *Tiger Woods*. Greensboro, NC: Morgan Reynolds, 1997.

Brewster, Todd, and Peter Jennings. *The Century for Young People.* New York: Random House, 1999.

Rowling, J. K. *Harry Potter and the Sorcerer's Stone.* New York: A. A. Levine Books, 1998.

Internet Links

http://www.nsync.com

http://www.magicjohnson.org

http://hubble.stsci.edu

For information about other U.S. subjects, type your key words into a search engine such as Alta Vista or Yahoo!

USA 1990s Index